TEN RUNGS

TEN RUNGS

HASIDIC SAYINGS

COLLECTED AND EDITED BY

MARTIN BUBER

SCHOCKEN BOOKS · NEW YORK

TRANSLATED BY OLGA MARX

First SCHOCKEN PAPERBACK edition 1962

10 9   85 86 87 88

Library of Congress Catalog Card No. 62-13135

Printed in the United States of America

ISBN 0-8032-0018-5

FOR THERE IS NO RUNG OF BEING

ON WHICH WE CANNOT FIND

THE HOLINESS OF GOD EVERYWHERE

AND AT ALL TIMES

They asked the "holy Yehudi": "Why is it written: 'Justice, justice, shalt thou follow' [Deut. 16:20]? Why is the word 'justice' repeated?"

He answered: "We ought to follow justice with justice, and not with unrighteousness." That means: The use of unrighteousness as a means to a righteous end makes the end itself unrighteous; injustice as a means to justice renders justice unjust.

What knowledge could be of greater importance to the men of our age, and to the various communities of our time? The saying sounds as if it were derived from the experiences of contemporaries. And yet it stems from the Napoleonic era, and was not spoken at the hub of events, but in a Polish ghetto, and by a *zaddik*, a "righteous man," who was a leader of *hasidim*, those "devout" souls who knew that no one can be really devout in relation to God, if he is not devout toward His creation, and that the love of God is unreal, unless it is crowned with love for one's fellow men.

This book contains a small selection of hasidic sayings of this nature. They all revolve around a single question: How can we fulfill the meaning of our existence on earth? And so, dear reader, these pages are not concerned with the mysteries of heaven, but with your life and mine, in this hour and the next. These sayings were scattered through hundreds of books, in versions largely distorted in the speeches and writings of the disciples who transmitted them. I have selected, reduced to the quintessence of meaning, and arranged them according to major themes, not because they are beautiful and interesting, but because of my belief that, in this selection, arrangement and form, they may serve to show even the reader who is very remote from their origins the way to the true life.

Jerusalem, 1947   Martin Buber

CONTENTS

THE RUNG OF GOD AND MAN

TWO KINDS OF FAITH

Why do we say: "Our God and the God of our fathers"?

There are two kinds of people who believe in God. One believes because he has taken over the faith of his fathers, and his faith is strong. The other has arrived at faith through thinking and studying. The difference between them is this: The advantage of the first is that, no matter what arguments may be brought against it, his faith cannot be shaken; his faith is firm because it was taken over from his fathers. But there is one flaw in it: he has faith only in response to the command of man, and he has acquired it without studying and thinking for himself. The advantage of the second is that, because he found God through much thinking, he has arrived at a faith of his own. But here too there is a flaw: it is easy to shake his faith by refuting it through evidence. But he who unites both kinds of faith is invincible. And so we say, "Our God" with reference to our studies, and "God of our fathers" with an eye to tradition.

The same interpretation has been given to our saying, "God of Abraham, God of Isaac, and God of Jacob," and not "God of Abraham, Isaac, and

Jacob," for this indicates that Isaac and Jacob did not merely take over the tradition of Abraham; they themselves searched for God.

SEEING AND BELIEVING

Question: It is written: "And Israel saw the great hand," and further on it is written: ". . . and they believed in the Lord, and in His servant Moses." Why is this said? The question as to whether or not one believes can only be put while one does not as yet "see."

Answer: You are mistaken. It is only then that the true question can be put. Seeing the great hand does not mean that faith can be dispensed with. It is only after "seeing" that one realizes what the lack of faith means, and feels how very much one needs faith. The seeing of the great hand is the beginning of faith in that which one cannot "see."

THE BEGINNING OF TEACHING

Rabbi Bunam began teaching with these words: "We thank You, who are blessed and who are the source of blessing, that you are manifest and hidden." Then he continued: "A fearless man must feel God as he feels the place on which he stands. And just as he cannot imagine himself without a place to stand on, so he must in all simplicity grow aware of God who is the Place of the world, and comprises it. But at the same time he must know that He is the hidden life which fills the world."

God says to man as he said to Moses: "Put off thy shoes from off thy feet"—put off the habitual which encloses your foot and you will recognize that the place on which you happen to be standing at this moment is holy ground. For there is no rung of being on which we cannot find the holiness of God everywhere and at all times.

THE WAY IN WHICH GOD HIDES

God hides in two ways. One way is that God hides so that it is very difficult to find him and yet he who knows that God is hiding from him can advance toward him and find him. The other way is that God hides from a man the fact that he is hiding and, since the seeker knows so little about God, he cannot find him. It is this that is referred to in the words: "I shall hide, hide." God hides the fact that he is hiding, and then those from whom he is hiding do not know him—the hidden one.

THE SHEPHERD IS THERE

It is written: "I saw all Israel scattered upon the mountains, as sheep that have no shepherd." This does not mean that the shepherd is not there. The shepherd is always there. But sometimes he hides, and then he is indeed not there to the sheep, because they do not see him.

BEYOND TIME

The understanding of man is not great enough to grasp the fact that God is beyond time. But you must understand that time exists only because we do not grasp it, only because our understanding is small. For the greater our understanding, the more time is on the wane. In a dream we live seventy years and discover, on awakening, that it was a quarter of an hour. In our life, which passes like a dream, we live seventy years and then we waken to a greater understanding which shows us that it was a quarter of an hour. With our small understanding we can never grasp what we will know with the greater. Perfect understanding is beyond time.

When the Messiah had learned what he learned since the creation of the world, and suffered what he suffered, God said to him: "Thou art My son, this day I have begotten thee."

WHO KNOWS ONE?

This is what Rabbi Moshe of Kobryn said concerning the first question in the game of riddles, sung at the end of the Passover Haggadah, "Who knows one? I know one":

"Who knows one?" said he. "Who can know the One? For even the seraphim ask: 'Where is the place of His glory?' And yet—'I know one.' For, as the sage says: 'Where shall I find you? . . . And where shall I not find you!' And the seraphim too reply: 'The whole earth is full of His glory.' By his works within me, I know the One."

THE STRONG THIEF

Every lock has its key which fits into and opens it. But there are strong thieves who know how to open locks without keys. They break the lock. So every mystery in the world can be unriddled by the particular kind of meditation fitted to it. But God loves the thief who breaks the lock open: I mean, the man who breaks his heart for God.

TWO KINDS OF FEAR

Question: When they stood at Mount Sinai, the people said to Moses: "Speak thou with us, and we will hear; but let not God speak with us, lest we die." And Moses answered: "Fear not." He went on to say that God had come "that His fear may be before you, that ye sin not." Is not that a contradiction?

Answer: "Fear not"—this means: this fear of

yours, the fear of death, is not the fear God wants
of you. He wants you to fear him, he wants you
to fear his remoteness, and not to fall into sin which
removes you from him.

OUR DISGRACE

Our disgrace is that we fear another besides
God. This is what was said of Jacob in the words:
"Then Jacob was greatly afraid and he was distressed." We must be distressed because of our
fear of Esau.

THE SOLITARY TREE

When I look at the world, it sometimes seems
to me as if every man were a tree in the wilderness, and God had no one in his world save him
alone, and he had none he could turn to, save God
alone.

A MAN ON EARTH

Question: Why is it written: "In the day that
God created *a man* on earth," and not "in the day
that God created *man* on earth"?

Answer: You shall serve your Creator as if
there were only one man in the world, only you
yourself.

THE DIVIDING WALL

In the Scriptures we read: "I stood between the
Lord and you." The "I" stands between God and

us. When a man says "I" and presumes to use his Maker's word, he is shutting himself off from him. But there is no dividing wall before him who sacrifices his "I." For of him it is written: "I am my beloved's, and his desire is toward me." When my "I" comes to belong to my beloved, then his desire is toward me.

WHO MAY BE CALLED MAN?

In the Scriptures we read: "When any man of you bringeth an offering unto the Lord ..." Only he who brings himself to God as an offering may be called man.

THE PUPIL

Rabbi Pinhas said: "Ever since I began giving true service to my Maker, I have not tried to gain anything, but only taken what God gave me. It is because the pupil is dark that it absorbs every ray of light."

HOLY DESPAIR

In the psalm we read: "How long shall I take counsel in my soul, having sorrow in my heart by day?"

As long as I take counsel in my soul, there must be sorrow in my heart all day. Only when I know of no further counsel that can help me, and I give up taking counsel, and know of no other help but God, will help be vouchsafed me.

Question: It is written: "I am JHWH, thy God, who brought thee out of the land of Egypt." Why does it not say: "I am JHWH, thy God, who created heaven and earth"?

Answer: "Heaven and earth!" Then man might have said, "Heaven—that's too much for me!" So God said to man: "I am the one who fished you out of the mud. Now you come here and listen to me!"

THE SHADOW

Man himself is the source of all his troubles, for the light of God pours over him eternally. But through his all-too-bodily existence man comes to cast a shadow, so that the light cannot reach him.

TWO KINDS OF LOVE FOR GOD

There are two kinds of love: the love of a man for his wife, which should manifest itself in secret and not where there are spectators, for this love can be consummated only in a place apart from other beings; and there is the love for one's brothers and sisters and children, a love which does not require secrecy.

And there are two kinds of love for God: the

love spent in learning and praying and fulfilling the commandments, which should be shown in silence and not in the presence of others, lest it tempt to glory and pride; and the love shown in the company of other human beings, when one hears and speaks, gives and takes, and, in one's secret heart, clings to God and never ceases dwelling upon him. And this love is on a higher rung than the other, and concerning it, we read: "Oh that thou wert as my brother, that sucked the breasts of my mother! When I should find thee without, I would kiss thee; yea and none would despise me."

TWO KINDS OF GOD'S LOVE

There are two kinds of love: one man loves whatever his clever son does and says, and boasts about his doing clever things and speaking clever words; the other loves his son for himself, no matter what he may say or do.

It is the same with the love of God for man. When a tried and proven man keeps the commandments and does good works wisely and well, God loves what he does and is present in all that he does, and thus the outer being of the universe is bound to God. But when the tried and proven man clings to God with his own being, then God loves him even when he does not work wisely and well, but goes his way with a simple mind and

clings to God. God loves him just for that reason.
And so the inner being of the universe is lifted to
God.

MOLTEN GODS

It is written: "Thou shalt make thee no molten
gods."

When you think of God, you should really
think of him, and not of a molten god which you
have made in your own image.

WE SHAPE A HUMAN FORM FOR GOD

Our sages said: "Know what is above you . . ."
The rabbi of Apt expounded this saying as follows:

" 'Know what is above you.' And what is this
that is above you? The prophet Ezekiel said: 'And
upon the likeness of the throne was a likeness as
the appearance of a man upon it above.' How can
this be said of God? For is it not written: 'To
whom then will ye liken Me, that I should be his
equal?' But the truth of the matter is that the 'likeness as the appearance of a man' is wrought by us.
It is the form we shape when we serve with true
and fervent hearts. Such service shapes a human
form for our Creator, to whom no one is like or
equal; it shapes him, blessed be he and blessed be
his name, in the semblance of man. When a man
is charitable and gives a service of love, he con-

tributes to the form of God's right hand. And when a man fights in the ranks of God and drives evil away, he contributes to the form of his left hand. He who is above you on the throne—his shape is your work."

WITH GOD

You must know that every movement you make is bound up with the will of the Creator. That is why it is written: "Noah walked with God." For every movement is made through the impulse given by God. Noah clung to God with such very great devotion that it seemed to him that, whenever he walked, God was moving his feet. At every step it seemed to him that God was facing him and guiding him as a father teaches his little son to walk, and when the father moves further away from him, the child knows it is for his own good.

SIGNS

This whole world is a cloak for the lowest rung of holiness, for its feet, as it were. As it is written: "And the earth is my footstool." God limits the godliness he has in infinity, and narrows it down to the focus of the material world in which man exists. And there he assigns every man his thought and word and deed according to the day, the place, and the person, and hides therein the signs to lead men to his service.

And so a man should immerse himself in the
task of understanding the signs which are cloaked
in thought and word and deed and so given to
him in particular, in his work and his affairs, and
in everything God appoints for him day by day.

CONCERNING SECRECY

Sometimes a man lies in bed, and the household
thinks he is asleep, but he is spending this hour in
solitude with his Maker, blessed be he. If the eyes
of his understanding can always behold his Maker
as if he were another human being—that is a very
high rung. And take this to heart: if at all times
you dwell in pure thoughts, then the Maker too
will look at you as though he were a human being.

FAITH

Faith is a very strong thing, and if a man has
faith and a simplicity that does not rationalize, he
will be found worthy of reaching the rung of
grace which is even higher than that of holy wisdom. He will be vouchsafed great and over-
whelming grace in God in very blissful silence,
until he will be able to bear the greatness of this
silence no longer, and will cry aloud out of the
fullness of his soul.

THE RUNG OF PRAYER

LET EVERYONE CRY OUT TO GOD

Let everyone cry out to God and lift his heart up to him, as if he were hanging by a hair, and a tempest were raging to the very heart of heaven, and he were at a loss for what to do, and there were hardly time to cry out. It is a time when no counsel, indeed, can help a man and he has no refuge save to remain in his loneliness and lift his eyes and his heart up to God, and cry out to him. And this should be done at all times, for in the world a man is in great danger.

THE SECRET PRAYER

This is how the words of prayer: "Hear us, when we call for help, hear our cries, Thou who knowest what is hidden," are expounded:

We do not even know how we are supposed to pray. All we do is call for help because of the need of the moment. But what the soul intends is spiritual need, only we are not able to express what the soul means. That is why we do not merely ask God to hear our call for help, but also beg him, who knows what is hidden, to hear the silent cry of the soul.

A king's son rebelled against his father and was banished from the sight of his face. After a time, the king was moved to pity for his fate and bade messengers go in search of him. It was long before one of the messengers found him—far from home. He was at a village inn, dancing barefoot and in a torn shirt in the midst of drunken peasants. The courtier bowed and said: "Your father has sent me to ask you what you desire. Whatever it may be, he is prepared to grant your wish." The prince began to weep. "Oh," said he, "if only I had warm clothing and a pair of stout shoes!"

See, that is how we whimper for the small needs of the hour and forget that the Glory of God is in exile!

FALSE PRAYER

He who prays in sorrow because of the bleakness which burdens his spirit, and thinks he is praying in the fear of God, or he who prays in joy because of the radiance in his spirit, and thinks he is praying in the love of God—his prayers are no good at all. For his fear is the burden of sadness, and his love is nothing but empty joy.

INTO THE WORD

You should utter words as though heaven were

opened within them and as though you did not put the word into your mouth, but as though you entered into the word.

OFFERING ONESELF UP

He who utters the word "Lord," and in doing so prepares to say "of the world," is not speaking as he should. At the moment he is saying "Lord," he must only think of offering himself up to the Lord, even if his soul perished in the Lord and he were not able to add the word "world." It should be enough for him to have been able to say "Lord."

EXCHANGE OF STRENGTH

When a Jew is about to say: "Blessed art thou, O Lord our God, King of the world," and prepares to utter the first word, the word "blessed," he shall do so with all his strength, so that he will have no strength left to say "art thou." And this is the meaning of the verse in the Scriptures: "But they that wait for the Lord shall exchange their strength." What we are really saying is: "Our Father in heaven, I am giving you all the strength that is within me in that very first word; now will you, in exchange, give me an abundance of new strength, so that I can go on with my prayer."

29

The psalm reads: "For singing to our God is good."

It is good if man can so bring it about that God sings within him.

THE RIGHT KIND OF ALTAR

It is written: "An altar of earth thou shalt make unto Me . . . and if thou make Me an altar of stone, thou shalt not build it of hewn stones, for if thou lift up thy tool upon it, thou hast profaned it."

The altar of earth is the altar of silence, which pleases God beyond all else. But if you do make an altar of words, do not hew and chisel them, for such artifice would profane it.

DISTURBANCE FROM WITHIN

To commune with your Maker in solitude and silence, to recite psalms and pray to him—this it is good to do with your whole heart, until you are overwhelmed with weeping and weep to God as a child weeps to its father. But to weep according to plan in the midst of prayer—that is unworthy! He who does so can no longer say what he says with a whole heart, and the truly great weeping will not overwhelm him. Even thoughts about prayer are like "alien thoughts" which hinder the soul from fixing itself wholly upon God.

There are people who can utter words of prayer with true fervor, so that the words shine like a precious stone whose radiance shines of itself. Then again there are people whose words are nothing but a window that has no light of its own, but only lets the light in and shines for that reason.

PRAYING AND EATING

Question: "Ye shall serve the Lord your God, and He will bless thy bread." Why is "ye" written first, and later "thy"?

Answer: To serve—that means to pray. When a man prays, and even if he does this alone in his room, he shall first unite with all of Israel; thus, in every true prayer, it is the community that is praying. But when one eats, and even if it is at a table full of people, each man eats for himself.

VALID PRAYER

A prayer which is not spoken in the name of all Israel is no prayer at all.

ALL THE MELODIES

Every people has its own melody, and no people sings the melody of another. But Israel sings all the melodies, in order to bring them to God. So, in the "Section of Praise," all the crea-

31

tures that live on the earth, and all the birds, utter each his own song. But Israel makes a song out of all of their songs, in order to bring them to God.

OF THE POWER OF THE WORD

When you speak, cherish the thought of the secret of the voice and the word, and speak in fear and love, and remember that the world of the word finds utterance through your mouth. Then you will lift the word.

Remember that you are only a vessel, and that your thought and your word are worlds that spread out: the world of the word—that is the Divine Presence which, when it is uttered, desires something from the world of thought. And when you have drawn the light of God into your thought and word, pray that something of the abundance and blessing from the world of thought may pour over the world of the word. Then you too will receive what you need. That is why we say: "Let us find you in our prayers!" God can be found in our very prayer.

HE IS YOUR PSALM

In the Scriptures we read: "He is thy psalm and He is thy God."

He is your psalm and he also is your God. The prayer a man says, that prayer, of itself, is God.

It is not as if you were asking something of a friend. Your friend is different from you and your words are different. It is not so in prayer, for prayer unites the principles. When a man who is praying thinks his prayer is something apart from God, he is like a suppliant to whom the king grants his request. But he who knows that prayer in itself is God is like the king's son who takes whatever he needs from the stores of his father.

THE RUNG OF HEAVEN AND EARTH

TWO WORLDS

The other nations, too, believe that there are two worlds. They, too, say, "in the world to come." The difference is this: they think that the two are separate and severed, but Israel professes that the two worlds are essentially one and shall, indeed, become one.

TO THE CHILDREN OF MEN

When Rabbi Enoch had said the verse of the psalm: "The heavens are the heavens of the Lord, but the earth hath He given to the children of men," he paused and then went on to say: " 'The heavens are the heavens of the Lord'—you see, they are already of a heavenly character. 'But the earth hath He given to the children of men'—so that they might make of it something heavenly."

IN THE DUST

Question: Why do people always weep when they say: "Man, his origin is of the dust and his end is in the dust"? If man sprang from gold and turned to dust, it would be proper to weep, but not if he returns whence he has come.

Answer: The origin of the world is dust, and

man has been placed in it that he may raise the dust to spirit. But his end is dust—and time and again it is the end where he fails, and everything crumbles into dust.

THE ZADDIKIM THAT BUILD

Question: How are we to interpret the words of our sages: "Every zaddik in whose day the Temple is not built, is no zaddik at all"? That would mean that all the zaddikim who have lived since the destruction of the Temple were not zaddikim.

Answer: The zaddikim are always building at the upper sanctuary. The zaddik who does not do his share in the building is no zaddik at all.

THE FIRST LIGHT

Before the soul enters the air of this world, it is conducted through all the worlds. Last of all, it is shown the first light which once—when the world was created—illuminated all things, and which God removed when mankind grew corrupt. Why is the soul shown this light? So that, from that hour on, it may yearn to attain the light, and approach it rung by rung in its life on earth. And those who reach it, the zaddikim—into them the light enters, and out of them it shines into the world again. That is the reason why it was hidden.

As the hand held before the eye hides the tallest mountain, so this small earthly life hides from our gaze the vast radiance and secrets of which the world is full, and whoever can take life from before his eyes, as one takes away one's hand, will see the great radiance within the world.

IN THE MIDST OF THE GARDEN

It is written: "The tree of life also in the midst of the garden." Whenever man studies or prays, he should think that he is in the garden of paradise, where there is no envy and no lust and no pride, and he will surely be safe from distraction. But how can he think in this way, since he knows that he is in this world and among people he is acquainted with? This is how: when man studies or prays with reverence and devoutness begotten of love, and fastens and binds his spirit to God and remembers that nothing is void of him and without him, but that everything is filled with life granted by the Creator, then, in all he sees, he sees the living power of the Creator and hears his living voice. That is the meaning of the words: "The tree of life in the midst of the garden." He who clings to the life of God is in the midst of the garden.

Man is always passing through two doors: out of this world and into the next, and out and in again.

THE LADDER

The souls descended from the realm of heaven to earth, on a long ladder. Then it was taken away. Now, up there, they are calling home the souls. Some do not budge from the spot, for how can one get to heaven without a ladder? Others leap and fall and leap again, and give up. But there are those who know very well that they cannot achieve it, but try and try over and over again until God catches hold of them and pulls them up.

EVERYTHING LEAVES TRACES

Man is a ladder placed on the earth and the top of it touches heaven. And all his movements and doings and words leave traces in the upper world.

ON THE EARTH

If a man of Israel has himself firmly in hand, and stands solidly on the earth, then his head reaches up to heaven.

ABRAHAM AND HIS GUESTS

Concerning Abraham, whom angels visited, the Scriptures say: "And he stood over them and they did eat." Why is this said in the Scriptures? It is not customary for the host who does not eat with his guests to stand over them while they eat. Now this is what is meant by these words in the Scriptures: The angels have their virtues and flaws, and men have their virtues and flaws. The virtue of angels is that they cannot deteriorate, and their flaw is that they cannot improve. Man's flaw is that he can deteriorate, and his virtue that he can improve. But a man who practices hospitality in the true sense of the word acquires the virtues of his guests. Thus Abraham acquired the virtue of angels who never deteriorate. And so he was over and above them.

TO WALK HIDDEN

It is written: "And to walk hidden with thy God." You know that angels stand. Ceaselessly they stand, each on his own rung, but we move, we move from rung to rung. For the angels are not garmented in flesh; they cannot remain hidden in the course of their service and no matter on what rung they stand, they are always manifest. But the son of man on earth is clothed with the stuff of earth and can hide within this body of his. And so—hidden from sight—he can move from rung to rung.

Why does God demand sacrifice of man and not of the angels? That of the angels would be purer than the service of man could ever be. But what God desires is not the deed but the preparation. The holy angels cannot prepare themselves; they can only do the deed. Preparation is the task of man who is caught in the thicket of tremendous obstacles, and must free himself. There is the advantage of the works of man.

AGAINST DEJECTION

In the psalm we read: "Who healeth the broken in heart . . ." Why are we told that? For it is a good thing to have a broken heart, and pleasing to God, as it is written: "The sacrifices of God are a broken spirit . . ." But further on in the psalm, we read: "And bindeth up their wounds." God does not entirely heal those who have broken hearts. He only eases their suffering, lest it torment and deject them. For dejection is not good and not pleasing to God. A broken heart prepares man for the service of God, but dejection corrodes service. We must distinguish between the two as carefully as between joy and wantonness; they are so easily confused, and yet are as far removed from one another as the ends of the earth.

We must not worry. Only one worry is permissible: a man should worry because he is worrying.

THE CHOICE

If we could hang all our sorrows on pegs and were allowed to choose those we liked best, everyone of us would take back his own, for all the rest would seem even more difficult to bear.

TRUE SORROW AND TRUE JOY

There are two kinds of sorrow and two kinds of joy. When a man broods over the misfortunes that have come upon him, when he cowers in a corner and despairs of help—that is a bad kind of sorrow, concerning which it is said: "The Divine Presence does not dwell in a place of dejection." The other kind is the honest grief of a man who knows what he lacks.

The same is true of joy. He who is devoid of inner substance and, in the midst of his empty pleasures, does not feel and does not try to fill his lack, is a fool. But he who is truly joyful is like a man whose house has burned down, who feels his need deep in his soul and begins to build anew. His heart rejoices over every stone that is laid.

ALL JOYS

All joys hail from the Garden of Eden, and jests too, provided they are uttered in true joy.

SORROW AND HAPPINESS

Happiness settles the spirit, but sorrow drives it into exile.

WHY THE REJOICING?

In the psalm we read: "Rejoice the soul of thy servant; for unto Thee, O Lord, do I lift up my soul." Why the rejoicing? "For unto Thee, O Lord, do I lift up my soul!" It is rejoicing which makes it possible for me to lift up my soul to you.

JOYLESS VIRTUE

If a man has fulfilled all the commandments, he is admitted to the Garden of Eden, even though he has not burned with fervor and has not experienced delight. But since he has felt no delight on earth, he feels none there either. Finally, he even grumbles: "And they make all that to-do about paradise!" And hardly have the words left his lips, when he is thrown out!

BETWEEN MEN

There are those who suffer very greatly and cannot tell what is in their hearts, and they go

their ways full of suffering. But if they meet someone whose face is bright with laughter, he can
quicken them with his gladness. And it is no small
thing to quicken a human being!

INTO GLADNESS

When people are merry and dance, it sometimes
happens that they catch hold of someone who is
sitting outside and grieving, pull him into the
round, and make him rejoice with them. The
same happens in the heart of one who rejoices:
grief and sorrow draw away from him, but it is a
special virtue to pursue them with courage and
to draw grief into gladness, so that all the strength
of sorrow may be transformed into joy.

THE RUNG OF SERVICE

THE NATURE OF SERVICE

This is the service man must perform all of his days: to shape matter into form, to refine the flesh, and to let the light penetrate the darkness, until the darkness itself shines and there is no longer any division between the two. As it is written: "And there was evening and there was morning, one day."

One should not make a great to-do about serving God. Does the hand boast when it carries out what the heart wills?

IMITATION OF THE FATHERS

Question: In the Book of Elijah we read: "Everyone of Israel is duty-bound to say: 'When will my works approach the works of my fathers, Abraham, Isaac and Jacob?'" How are we to understand this? How could we ever venture to think that we could do what our fathers did?

Answer: Just as our fathers invented new ways of serving, each a new service according to his own character: one, the service of love; another, of stern justice; a third, of beauty; so each one of us in his own way should devise something new in the light of the teaching and of service, and do what has not yet been done.

49

Question: Rashi expounds the words of God: "I appeared unto Abraham, unto Isaac, and unto Jacob" as meaning "I appeared to the fathers." In what way can this be considered an explanation?

Answer: He who had a father who was righteous and devout is not apt to make a great effort to perfect himself, for he leans on the merits of his father. This is even more true of one whose father and grandfather were both holy men; the mere fact that he is their grandson seems to him like solid ground beneath his feet. But this was not so in the days of the patriarchs: Isaac did not concern himself with the merit his father had acquired, nor Jacob with that of his father and his ancestors, for they did not want to be grandsons, but fathers.

EACH HIS OWN

When a man leaves his own rung and takes that of his friend, he will not be fruitful on either the one rung or the other. Many followed the example of Rabbi Simeon ben Yohai, and their work did not succeed because they were not of his quality, but only did as he did, in imitation of his quality.

ORIGINALITY

When a man embarks on something great, in the spirit of truth, he need not be afraid that another may imitate him. But if he does not do so in the spirit of truth, but plans to act in a way that no one else can imitate, then he drags the great down to the lowest level—and everyone can do the same.

THE GATE

It is written: "Open to me the gates of right-eousness."

Man is serving in the right way as long as he feels that he is still on the outside and begs God to open the gate to true service for him.

ONLY A BEGINNING

A man ought never to say that he is perfect in his fear of God; he should always say that now he is only about to begin to serve God. For did not Moses, after forty years of wandering, say to God: "Thou hast begun to show Thy servant Thy greatness"? And that is why it is written: "As a beginning God created the heaven and the earth." He created all in heaven and all on earth as a beginning of the fear of God, as a beginning of the knowledge of him.

RENEWAL

In order to perfect oneself, one must renew oneself day by day.

NEW EVERY MORNING

Unless we believe that God renews the work of

creation every day, our prayers and doing the commandments grow old and accustomed and tedious. As it is written in the psalm: "Cast me not off in the time of old age"—that is to say, do not let my world grow old.

And in Lamentations it is written: "They are new every morning: great is Thy faithfulness." The fact that the world is new to us every morning—that is your great faithfulness!

THE MANIFEST AND THE SECRET

The two things that Israel stated on Horeb: "We will do and obey," represent what is manifest in the teachings and the commandments, what can and should be done, as well as the mystery which surrounds the teachings and the commandments, the mystery which is not revealed within them, which we become conscious of only when we pray. And this we grow aware of in prayer only when our prayers cling to the boundless. The two exist in every world; everyone has both, each according to his rung.

And he who rises to a higher rung converts his obeying into doing, and then is given a new "we obey," and so on from rung to rung. The same holds for the worlds. What in this, our world, is a "we obey," is a "we do" for the world of heavenly spheres, and the heavens have a higher "we obey," and so on from world to world.

VALID SACRIFICE

It is written: "And Abel, he also brought." The "he" is what he brought: he brought himself. Only when a man brings himself, too, is his sacrifice valid.

WITH DIFFERENT INTENT

This was Rabbi Uri's comment on the story in the Midrash, that when young Abraham refused to serve idols and was thrown into the fire, he did not burn to death:

"Abraham thought: 'If I want the idols to be thrown into the fire, I myself must go into the fire.' That is why he survived. But his brother Haran thought: 'As soon as I see that nothing happens to Abraham, I too will give myself up.' That is why he burned to death."

TO DIE AND TO LIVE

It is written in the psalm: "I shall not die, but live." In order really to live, man must first give himself to death. But when he has done so, he discovers that he is not to die, that he is to live.

IN ALL WAYS

Man should serve God with all his strength, for all of it is needed. God wants us to serve him in all ways.

And this is what is meant:

It sometimes happens that a man takes a walk

and talks with one person or another. And since, during this time, he cannot study, he should cling to God and join the Names of God with his soul. And when a man goes on a journey and cannot pray as usual, he should serve God in other ways. Let him not grieve because of this, for God wants us to serve him in all ways, now in this way and now in that way, and it is he who bade the man talk to people or undertake a journey, so that God might be served in these ways as well.

FULFILMENT

This is the secret of the unity of God: no matter where I take hold of a shred of it, I hold the whole of it. And since the teachings and all the commandments are radiations of his being, he who lovingly does one commandment utterly and to the core, and in this one commandment takes hold of a shred of the unity of God, holds the whole of it in his hand, and has fulfilled all.

THE WAY

It is impossible to tell men what way they should take. For one way to serve God is by the teachings, another by prayer, another way by fasting, and still another by eating. Everyone should carefully observe which way his heart draws him, and then choose that way with all his strength.

INFINITY

Infinity shall be contained in every deed of man, in his speaking and seeing, listening and walking, standing still and lying down.

ADAM'S SIN

Question: What was Adam's real sin?

Answer: Adam's real sin was that he worried about the morrow. The serpent set out to reason with him: "There is no service you can perform, for you cannot distinguish between good and evil and are unable to make a choice. Eat of this fruit and you will be able to distinguish; you will choose the good and receive your reward." That he gave ear to this—that is where Adam was at fault. He worried that he would not be able to serve, yet at that very hour he had his service: to obey God and to resist the serpent.

THE TEN PRINCIPLES

Said the Great Maggid to Rabbi Zusya, his disciple: "I cannot teach you the ten principles of service. But a little child and a thief can show you what they are.

"From the child you can learn three things:
    He is merry for no particular reason;
    Never for a moment is he idle;
    When he needs something, he demands it vigorously.

"The thief can instruct you in seven things:
   He does his service by night;
   If he does not finish what he has set out to do
      in one night, he devotes the next night to it;
   He and those who work with him love one
      another;
   He risks his life for slight gains;
   What he takes has so little value for him that
      he gives it up for a very small coin;
   He endures blows and hardship, and it mat-
      ters nothing to him;
   He likes his trade and would not exchange
      it for any other."

PARTICIPATION

This was Rabbi Mikhal's comment on the words of Hillel, "If I am not for myself, who will be for me? And if I am for myself, what am I?":

" 'If I am not for myself,' that is, if I do not work for myself alone, but continually participate in the congregation, 'who will be for me?' In that case, whatever 'who,' that is, whatever any member of the congregation does in my place, counts just as though I had done it myself. But if I am 'for myself'—if I do not participate with others, if I do not join with them—'what am I?' Then everything in the way of good works which I have wrought alone is less than nothing in the eyes of God, who is the source of all good."

56

THE RUNG OF THE TEACHINGS

UNTO THE HEART OF HEAVEN

This is how Rabbi Enoch interpreted the words in the Scriptures, ". . . and the mountain burned with fire unto the heart of heaven":

"The fire of Sinai burned into the core of men until it made something heavenly of their hearts."

THE TRUE EXODUS

Question: The Feast of Weeks was really instituted to commemorate Revelation, so why does one speak of it as being "in commemoration of the exodus from Egypt"?

Answer: Did not God speak to Moses out of the burning bush, saying: "And this shall be the token unto thee, that I have sent thee: when thou hast brought forth the people out of Egypt, ye shall serve God upon this mountain"? Their receiving the Torah at Sinai was the sign that they were out of Egypt. Up to that time, they were still caught in the bondage of Egypt.

EVERY DAY

Everyone of Israel is told to think of himself as standing at Mount Sinai to receive the Torah.

For man there are past and future events, but not so for God: day in, day out, he gives the Torah.

THE ETERNAL VOICE

Of the voice over Sinai, the Scriptures say that "it went on no more." According to the Aramaic translation, this means that the voice never paused at all. And the voice does, indeed, speak today, just as it did in times immemorial. But just as then, now too, one requires preparation to be able to hear it. As it is written: "Now, therefore, if ye will hearken, hearken to my voice." The word "now" means at whatever moment we hear it.

GIVING AND RECEIVING

Question: Why is the Feast of Revelation designated as the time we were given the Torah rather than the time we received the Torah?

Answer: The giving took place on the day commemorated by this feast, but the receiving takes place at all times. It was given to all equally, but they did not all receive in equal measure.

DREAMS

Dreams are a secretion of our thoughts and through them our thought is purified. All the wisdom in the world is a secretion of the Torah, and through it the Torah is purified. That is why we read: "When the Lord brings back those that returned to Zion, we will be like unto them that dream." For then it will be revealed that wisdom exists only that the Torah may be purified, and exile only that the thought of Israel may be purified, and all will be as a dream.

THE CHAIN

The zaddik cannot speak words of teaching unless he first links his soul to the soul of his dead teacher or to that of his teacher's teacher. Only then is link welded to link, and the teachings flow from Moses to Joshua, from Joshua to the Elders, and so on to the zaddik's own teacher, and from his teacher to him.

HOW WE SHOULD LEARN

Question: How can a man ever learn the Talmud adequately? For there we find that Abbayyi said this, and Raba said that. It is just as if Abbayyi were of one world and Raba of quite another. How is it possible to understand and learn both at the same time?

Answer: He who wants to understand Abbayyi's words must link his soul to the soul of Abbayyi; then he will learn the true meaning of the words as Abbayyi himself utters them. And, after that, if he wants to understand Raba's words, he must link his soul to the soul of Raba. That is what is meant in the Talmud when we read: "When a word is spoken in the name of its speaker, his lips move in the grave." And the lips of him who utters the word move like those of the master who is dead.

NO MORE THAN THIS

Question: It is written: "And ye shall be unto Me a kingdom of priests, and a holy nation. These are the words which thou shalt speak unto the children of Israel." Rashi, our teacher, comments: "These are the words, no more and no less." What does he mean by that?

Answer: Moses was good. He wanted to reveal more to the people, but he was not allowed. For it was God's will that the people make an effort of their own. Moses was to say just these words to them, no more and no less, so that they might feel: Something is hidden here, and we must strive to discover it for ourselves. That is why, further on, we read: "And he set before them all these words." No more and no less.

ETERNAL BEGINNINGS

Question: The Talmud teaches that: "Those who are perfect in righteousness cannot stand in that place where they stand who turn to God." According to this, one who has been free of sin from youth comes after one who has transgressed against God many times, and cannot attain the latter's rung.

Answer: He who sees a new light every day, light he did not see the day before, if he wishes truly to serve, must condemn his imperfect service of yesterday, atone for it, and start again. The person who is free of sin, who believes he has done perfect service and persists in that belief, does not accept the light, and comes after him who is ever turning again.

THE MAN WHO DENIES GOD

Whoever says that the words of the Torah are one thing and the words of the world another must be regarded as a man who denies God.

NO GRAVEN IMAGE

It is written: "Take heed unto yourselves, lest ye forget the covenant of the Lord your God, which He made with you, and make you a graven image, even the likeness of anything which the Lord thy God hath bidden thee," and not—as the meaning really demands—"which the Lord thy God hath forbidden thee."

"The Torah warns us," said the zaddik who had been listening, "not to make a graven image of anything the Lord our God has bidden us."

Our sages very properly emphasize that in the first psalm the Torah is called "the law of the Lord," and later "His Torah." For if a man learns the Torah for its own sake, then it is given to him, and it is his, and he may clothe all his holy thoughts in the holy Torah.

UPON THY HEART

"And these words which I command thee this day, shall be upon thy heart." The verse does not say: "in thy heart." For there are times when the heart is shut. But the words lie upon the heart, and when the heart opens in holy hours, they sink deep down into it.

LEARN FROM ALL

Question: In the *Sayings of the Fathers* we read: "Who is wise? He who learns from all men, as it is said, 'From all my teachers I have gotten understanding.'" Then why does it not say: "He who learns from every teacher"?

Answer: The master who pronounced this dictum is intent on making it clear that we can learn not only from those whose occupation is to teach but from every man. Even from a person who is ignorant, or from one who is wicked, you can gain understanding as to how to conduct your life.

"You can learn from everything," the rabbi of Sadagora once said to his hasidim. "Everything can teach us something, and not only everything God has created. What man has made has also something to teach us."

"What can we learn from a train?" one hasid asked dubiously.

"That because of one second one can miss everything."

"And from the telegraph?"

"That every word is counted and charged."

"And the telephone?"

"That what we say here is heard there."

THE SOUL'S TEACHING

Rabbi Pinhas often cited the words: "A man's soul will teach him," and emphasized them by adding: "There is no man who is not constantly being taught by his soul."

One of his disciples asked: "If this is so, why don't men obey their souls?"

"The soul teaches constantly," Rabbi Pinhas explained, "but it never repeats."

HOW TO SAY TORAH

I shall teach you the best way to say Torah. You must cease to be aware of yourselves. You must be nothing but an ear that hears what the universe of the word is constantly saying within you. The moment you start hearing what you yourself are saying, you must stop.

TO SAY TORAH AND BE TORAH

This is what Rabbi Leib, son of Sarah, used to say about those rabbis who expound the Torah:

"What does it amount to—their expounding the Torah! A man should see to it that all his actions are a Torah and that he himself becomes so entirely a Torah that one can learn from his habits and his motions and his motionless clinging to God."

THE RUNG OF THE WAY

THE WORLD

The world is a spinning die, and everything turns and changes: man is turned into angel, and angel into man, and the head into the foot, and the foot into the head. Thus all things turn and spin and change, this into that, and that into this, the topmost to the undermost, and the undermost to the topmost. For at the root all is one, and salvation inheres in the change and return of things.

THE WAY OF LIFE

The way in this world is like the edge of a blade. On this side is the underworld, and on that side is the underworld, and the way of life lies between.

TRUE JUSTICE

It is written: "Justice, justice shalt thou follow." For when a man believes that he is wholly just and need not strive further, then justice does not recognize him. You must follow justice and never stand still, and in your own eyes you must always be like a new-born child that has not yet achieved anything at all—for that is true justice.

69

God said to Abraham: "Get thee out of thy country, and from thy kindred, and from thy father's house, unto the land that I will show thee." God says to man: "First, get you out of your country, that means the dimness you have inflicted on yourself. Then out of your birthplace, that means out of the dimness your mother inflicted on you. After that, out of the house of your father, that means out of the dimness your father inflicted on you. Only then will you be able to go to the land that I will show you."

THE UNITY OF QUALITIES

The words in the Scriptures: "But ye that did cleave unto the Lord your God are alive every one of you this day," are expounded as follows:

"Cleave to his qualities." But this must be properly understood. Emanating from God are ten qualities and these come in twos which oppose each other like two colors, one of which is apparently in direct contrast to the other. But, seen with the true inner eye, they all form one simple unity. It is the task of man to make them appear a unity to the true outer eye, as well. Perhaps one man finds it difficult to be merciful, because his way is to be rigorous, and another finds it difficult to be rigorous, because his way is merciful. But he who binds the rigor within him to its root, to the rigor of God, and the mercy which is in him to its root, to the mercy of God, and so on in all things—such a man will unite the ten qualities within himself, and he himself will become the unity they represent, for he cleaves to the Lord of the world. Such a man has become wax on which both judgment and mercy can set their seal.

ASCENT

No limits are set to the ascent of man, and to each and everyone the highest stands open. Here it is only your personal choice that decides.

THE WILL AND THE STUMBLING BLOCK

There is no stumbling block one cannot push aside, for the stumbling block is only there for the sake of the will, and there actually are no stumbling blocks save in the spirit.

BODY AND SOUL

Everyone should have pity upon his body and allow it to share in all that illumines the soul. We must purify the body very greatly so that it may share in everything the soul receives, so that there may be a change in the present state where the soul attains to lofty matters and the body knows nothing about them. But if the body is given a share, it can also be of use to the soul. For, at times, the soul falls from its rung, and then the purified body can help it up again through the power of the light it has absorbed. That is why Job says: "From out my flesh shall I see God."

THE TEST

Question: Why is the sacrifice of Isaac considered so glorious? At that time, our Father Abraham had already reached a high rung of holiness, and so it was no wonder that he immediately did as God asked him!

Answer: When man is tried, all the rungs and all holiness are taken from him. Stripped of everything he has attained, he stands face to face with God who is putting him to the test.

THE MOUTH AND THE HEART

Our sages say: "Micah came and reduced the number of the commandments to three," that is, he supported the law by the three pillars on which the world rests: "to do justly"—that is justice; "to love mercy"—that is charity; "to walk humbly with thy God"—that is the central pillar, the order of truth: that your heart and mouth be one and not directed to devious purposes, nor to any of the evil powers which are called "the dead." That is why our sages say, "to walk humbly"—this refers to escorting the dead, and bringing in the bride. First the dead, the powers of evil are led out, and then in comes the bride. For he who joins his mouth and his heart, joins the bridegroom and the bride—God who is holy, with his Presence.

WITHIN AND WITHOUT

Man is afraid of things that cannot harm him, and he knows it; and he craves things that cannot help him, and he knows it. But actually, it is something within man he is afraid of, and it is something within man that he craves.

JUDGING ONESELF

If a man does not judge himself, all things will judge him, and all things will become messengers of God.

JUDGMENT

He who desires to become aware of the hidden light must lift the feeling of fear up to its source. And he can accomplish this if he judges himself and all he does. For then he sheds all fears and lifts fear that has fallen down. But if he does not judge himself, he will be judged from on high, and this judgment will come upon him in the guise of countless things, and all the things in the world will become messengers of God who carry out the judgment on this man.

There are two kinds of spirit, and they are like backward and forward. There is a spirit man attains to in the course of time. But there is also a spirit which overwhelms man with great abundance, in great haste, swifter than the fleeting moment, for it is beyond time, and for this spirit the element of time is not needed.

PREGNANCY

When a man grows aware of a new way in which to serve God, he should carry it around with him secretly, and without uttering it, for nine months, as though he were pregnant with it, and let others know of it only at the end of that time, as though it were a birth.

THE GROWING TREE

Man is like a tree. If you stand in front of a tree and watch it incessantly, to see how it grows, and to see how much it has grown, you will see nothing at all. But tend it at all times, prune the runners and keep it free of beetles and worms, and— all in good time—it will come into its growth. It is the same with man: all that is necessary is for him to overcome his obstacles, and he will thrive and grow. But it is not right to examine him hour after hour to see how much has already been added to his stature.

Question: It is written: "And this is the bless-ing, wherewith Moses, the man of God, blessed the children of Israel before his death." Of the words "before his death," Rashi says: "just before his death" and, in support of this interpretation, adds: "If not then, then when?" In what way does this mean more than what anyone can glean from the Scriptures?

Answer: Note that this is the only passage in which Moses is called a "man of God." Now this is how it was: because of his great love for Israel, Moses had long wanted to bless them, time and again. But each time he felt he would reach a higher rung, and that his blessing would then have greater strength, and that was why he delayed giving it. But when he had reached the rung of "the man of God," that is, the rung of the angels who do not move from rung to rung like men, but remain fixed, he knew that he must be very close to death, and then he blessed Israel.

HE WHO HAS A HEART

He who has a heart, is not concerned with space and place, for he himself is the place of the world. For God is in one's heart, as we read in the psalm: "God is the rock of my heart." And God speaks to Moses: "Behold, there is a place by Me." We know that God is the place of the world and that it is not the world which is his place. And the same holds for him who has a heart, since God is in his heart. He whose heart is the heart of Israel must not say: "This place does not suit me," for place and space cannot matter to him, because he is the place of the world, and the world is not his place.

THE RUNG OF LOVE

HIDING AND REVELATION

When senseless hatred reigns on earth, and men hide their faces from one another, then heaven is forced to hide its face. But when love comes to rule the earth, and men reveal their faces to one another, then the splendor of God will be revealed.

LETTERS AND SOULS

The myriads of letters in the Torah stand for the myriads of souls in Israel. If one single letter is left out of the Torah, it becomes unfit for use; if one single soul is left out of the union of Israel, the Divine Presence will not rest upon it. Like the letters, so the souls must unite and form a union. But why is it forbidden for one letter in the Torah to touch its neighbor? Because every soul of Israel must have hours when it is alone with its Maker.

IN WATER

Question: It is written in Proverbs: "As in water face answereth to face, so the heart of man to man." Why does the verse read "in water" and not "in a mirror"?

Answer: Man can see his reflection in water only when he bends close to it, and the heart of man too must lean down to the heart of his fellow; then it will see itself within his heart.

GIVE AND TAKE

The motto of life is: "Give and Take." Everyone must be both a giver and a receiver. Who is not both is as a barren tree.

IN EVERY MAN

In every man there is something precious, which is in no one else. And so we should honor each for what is hidden within him, for what only he has, and none of his comrades.

THE DARKNESS OF THE SOUL

It is written: "They saw not one man his brother, neither rose any from his place." He who will not look at his brother will soon come to this: He will cleave to his place and not be able to move from it.

OUR TEST

Everything in the world can be examined by its own particular test, to see if it is as it should be. And what is the test for the man of Israel? It is his love for Israel. When he sees that love for Israel grows greater in his soul day by day, he knows that he is ascending in the service of God.

CONCERNING THE STORK

In the Talmud it says that the stork is called *hasidah* in Hebrew, i.e., the devout or the loving one, because he gives so much love to his mate and his young. Then why is he classed in the Scriptures among the unclean birds? Because he gives love only to his own.

THE COMMANDMENT TO LOVE

Question: We are commanded to love our neighbor as ourselves. How can I do this if my neighbor has wronged me?

Answer: You must understand these words rightly. Love your neighbor as something which you yourself are. For all souls are one. Each is a spark from the original soul, and this soul is inherent in all souls, just as your soul is inherent in all the members of your body. It may come to pass that your hand will make a mistake and strike you. But would you then take a stick and chastise your hand because it lacked understanding, and so increase your pain? It is the same if your neighbor, who is of one soul with you, wrongs you because of his lack of understanding. If you punish him, you only hurt yourself.

Question: But if I see a man who is wicked before God, how can I love him?

Answer: Don't you know that the primordial

soul came out of the essence of God, and that every human soul is a part of God? And will you have no mercy on man, when you see that one of his holy sparks has been lost in a maze and is almost stifled?

LOVE OF ENEMIES

Rabbi Mikhal gave this command to his sons: "Pray for your enemies that all may be well with them. And should you think this is not serving God, rest assured that, more than all our prayers, this love is indeed the service of God."

NO BARRIER

We should also pray for the wicked among the peoples of the world; we should love them too. As long as we do not pray in this way, as long as we do not love in this way, the Messiah will not come.

THE TRUE LOVE OF GOD

To love God truly, one must first love man. And if anyone tells you that he loves God and does not love his fellow-man, you will know that he is lying.

THE ROOT

Everyone of Israel is rooted in our union, and so we must not thrust him from us completely;

for he who thrusts his neighbor away is thrusting himself away. And even more: he who thrusts away even the smallest jot of the whole, is thrusting all of the whole away from himself.

AS YOURSELF

What you must do is love your neighbor as yourself. There is no one who knows your many faults better than you! But you love yourself notwithstanding. And so you must love your neighbor, no matter how many faults you see in him.

ACCUSATION AND JUSTIFICATION

When you accuse a sinner and pronounce judgment upon him, saying that he deserves such and such a misfortune, you are pronouncing judgment upon yourself. Though the trespass of the other may be alien to your soul, you must have trespassed in some such way yourself. If you accuse him of idol worship, for example, you have probably been guilty of pride, and that is just as if you yourself had served an idol. And your guilt may even be greater. For you are subject to sterner judgment. But if you justify the sinner and point to the fact that he is still prisoned in his flesh and cannot govern his urges, then you are justifying yourself.

Question: Our sages say: "And there is not a thing that has not its place." And so man too has his place. Then why do people sometimes feel so crowded?

Answer: Because each wants to occupy the place of the other.

THE MOTIVE

Question: God asked Cain why his face had fallen. What does that mean? How could his face not "fall," since God had not accepted his gift!

Answer: God asked Cain: "Why is thy face thus fallen? Because I did not accept your gift, or because I accepted that of your brother?"

WHEN TWO SING

When a man is singing and cannot lift his voice, and another comes and sings with him, another who can lift his voice, the first will be able to lift his voice too. That is the secret of the bond between spirits.

CLIMBING DOWN

If you want to raise a man from mud and filth, do not think it is enough to stay on top and reach a helping hand down to him. You must go all the way down yourself, down into mud and filth.

Then take hold of him with strong hands and pull him and yourself out into the light.

WHEN IT IS GOOD
TO DENY THE EXISTENCE OF GOD

There is no quality and there is no power in man that was created to no purpose. And even base and corrupt qualities can be uplifted to serve God. When, for example, self-assurance is uplifted, it changes into proud assurance of the ways of God. But to what end can the denial of God have been created? It too can be uplifted through deeds of charity. For if someone comes to you and asks your help, you shall not turn him off with pious words, saying: "Have faith and take your troubles to God!" You shall act as though there were no God, as though there were only one person in all the world who could help this man—only yourself.

THE RUNG OF GOOD AND EVIL

EVIL

Question: The Talmud says that the child in the womb of his mother looks from one end of the world to the other and knows all the teachings, but that the instant he comes in contact with the air of earth an angel strikes him on the mouth, and he forgets everything. I do not understand why this should be: why first know everything and then forget it?

Answer: A trace is left behind in man through which he can reacquire the knowledge of the world and the teachings, and do God's service.

Question: But why must the angel strike man? If he did not, there would be no evil.

Answer: But if there were no evil, there would be no good, for good is the counterpart of evil. Everlasting delight is no delight. That is how we must interpret what we are taught: that the creation of the world took place for the good of its creatures. And that is why it is written: "It is not good that the man"—that is to say the primal man God created—"should be alone," that is, without the countereffect and the hindrance of the Evil Inclination, as was the case before the creation of the world. For there is no good unless its counterpart exists. And further on we read: "I will make him a help meet for him"—the fact that evil confronts good gives man the possibility of victory: of rejecting evil and choosing good. Only then does the good exist truly and perfectly.

THE EXILE OF THE DIVINE PRESENCE

The Divine Presence governs from top to bottom and to the verge of all rungs. That is the secret hidden in the words: "And Thou preservest them all." Even when a man sins, his sin is encompassed by the Presence because without it he would not have the power to move a limb. And that is the exile of the Divine Presence.

THE LOWEST RUNG

In the story of the Creation we read: ". . . and behold, it was very good." But, in the passage where Moses reproves Israel, the verse says: "See, I have set before thee this day life and good, and death and evil." Where did the evil come from?

Evil too is good. It is the lowest rung of perfect goodness. If you do good deeds, even evil will become good; but if you sin, evil will really become evil.

THE THRONE

The Divine Presence comprises all worlds, all creatures, good and evil. It is true unity. How then can it contain good and evil, which are self-contradictory? But actually there is no contradiction, for evil is the throne of good.

UNIFICATION

Just as all worlds, the good and the evil, are comprised in the Divine Presence, so they were comprised in Moses. When God spoke to Moses for the first time, he did not answer: "Here I am," because he was stricken with wonder: how can unification come to pass? For when God revealed himself in the thorn-bush, that is to say, in evil, in the lowest rung, all the wells of fire gushed forth from the summit down to the depths—yet the thorn-bush did not burn; evil was not consumed. How could this be? But God called a second time: "Moses!" And then the lowest and the highest rung linked within Moses himself, and he said: "Here I am."

COUNTRY HOUSES

God's relationship to the wicked may be compared to that of a prince who, besides his magnificent palaces, owns all manner of little houses hidden away in the woods and in villages, and visits them occasionally to hunt or to rest. The dignity of a palace is no greater than that of such a temporary abode, for the two are not alike, and what the lesser accomplishes the greater cannot. It is the same with the righteous man. Though his value and service may be great, he cannot accomplish what the wicked man accomplishes in the hour when he prays or does something to honor God, and God who is watching the worlds of confusion rejoices in him. That is why the righteous man should not consider himself better than the wicked.

AFAR OFF

It is written: "Am I a God near at hand . . . and not a God afar off?" "Afar off" refers to the wicked. "Near at hand" refers to the righteous. God says: "Do I want him who is already close to me, do I want the righteous? Why, I also want him who is afar off, I want him who is wicked!"

HOW GOD LOVES

If only I could love the greatest zaddik as much as God loves the worst ne'er-do-well!

WAYS

Question: It is written: ". . . for the Lord regardeth the way of the righteous; but the way of the wicked shall perish." The two parts of this sentence do not seem to belong together.

Answer: The righteous have many and devious

ways, and the wicked have also many and devious ways. But the Lord knows the ways of the righteous, because they are all one way and that is the way. But the ways of the wicked are numerous and manifold, for they are nothing but many ways of losing the one way. And in the end they themselves realize that each is losing his way and all ways, as when someone is walking through a wood and keeping to a certain way, though he does not know why he has taken that particular way rather than another. Day and night he keeps walking until he comes to a tall beech standing at the end; and, at that point the way is lost. The man cannot go forward and he does not dare go back, for he has lost the way.

THE "WAY" OF THE WICKED

It is written: "Let the wicked forsake his way." Does the wicked have a way? What he has is a mire, not a way. Now what is meant is this: let the wicked leave his "way," that is, his illusion of having a way.

FREEDOM OF CHOICE

It is God's will that there be freedom of choice. That is why he has waited until this day. For, in the days of the Temple, they had the death penalty and whipping, and so there was no freedom of choice. Afterwards, Israel had penal codes, so there was still no freedom of choice. But now everyone can sin openly and without shame, and live and prosper. And so, whoever leads a good life today is worthy in the eyes of God, and it is he who will bring about salvation.

THE TRICKERY OF THE EVIL INCLINATION

The Evil Inclination is like one who runs about the world keeping his hand closed. Nobody knows what he has inside of it. He goes up to everyone and asks: "What do you suppose I have in my hand?" And every person thinks that just what he wants most of all is hidden there. And everyone runs after the Evil Inclination. Then he opens his hand, and it is empty.

THE WORST

Rabbi Shelomo asked: "What is the worst thing the Evil Inclination can achieve?" And he answered: "To make man forget that he is the son of a king."

STRATEGIC RETREAT

Rabbi Abraham said:

"I have learned a new form of service from the wars of Frederick, king of Prussia. It is not necessary to approach the enemy in order to attack him. In fleeing from him, it is possible to circumvent him as he advances and fall on him from the rear and force him to surrender. What is needed is not to strike straight at evil but to withdraw to the sources of divine power, and from there to circle around evil, bend it and transform it into its opposite."

A GREAT ADVANTAGE

He who still harbors an Evil Inclination has a great advantage, for he can serve God with it. He can gather all his passion and warmth and pour them into the service of God. He who has no Evil Inclination at all cannot give perfect service. What counts is to restrain the blaze in the hour of desire and let it flow into the hours of prayer and service.

THE OFFERING

It is written: ". . . of every man whose heart maketh him willing ye shall take My offering." Every man should take the goodness with which he is to serve God out of all his heart's promptings, out of his cravings and desires, out of all his urge's drivings. If he is seized with love or fear, let him take this love or fear and use it to love and to fear God. Had Esau gone in the way of the teachings, his service would have been better than Jacob's, for he would have lifted all his evil passions up to God.

In the righteous the Evil Inclination changes into a holy angel, into a being that yields power and destiny.

THE MOUNTING

It is written: "Let us take our journey, and let us go, and I will go before thee." That is what the Evil Inclination says to a man secretly. For it is an inclination to become good and wants to become good by driving man to overcome it, and to make it good. And this is the secret request the Evil Inclination makes to the man he is trying to seduce: "Let us leave this disgraceful state and take service with the Creator, so that I too may go and mount with you rung by rung, although I seem to oppose, to disturb, and hinder you."

GREAT GUILT

He who learns the Torah and is not troubled by it, who sins and forgives himself, who prays because he prayed yesterday—the worst scoundrel is better than he!

THE ALPHABET

Question: Why, on the Day of Atonement, is the confession of sins given in alphabetical order?

Answer: If it were otherwise we should not

know when to stop beating our breast. For there is no end to sin, and no end to the awareness of sin, but there *is* an end to the alphabet.

THE THREE QUESTIONS

The rabbi of Ger was expounding the Scriptures, and came to the words Jacob says to his servant: "When Esau my brother meeteth thee, and asketh thee, saying: 'Whose art thou? and whither goest thou? and whose are these before thee?' " He said to his disciples: "Note how much Esau's questions resemble the saying of the sages: 'Reflect upon three things: know whence you have come, and where you are going, and before whom you will some time have to give account and reckoning.' Note it well, for he who reflects on these three things needs much self-examination, lest Esau ask within him. For Esau too can ask about these three, and bring heaviness into the heart of man."

UNMIXED

The important thing is not to mix the good with the bad. A mere touch of goodness suffices, if only it has not the slightest trace of admixture.

GREAT HOLINESS

There is many a great zaddik, so great that the world could not endure his holiness. And so he hides it far away, and nothing about him seems particularly holy or remote. He is like the Song of Songs, of which it is said: "All songs are holy; the Song of Songs is the Holy of Holies." King Solomon composed three books, two of which, Proverbs and Ecclesiastes, are full of moral sayings and the fear of God, and in them there is much talk of purity and devoutness. But in the Song of Songs such words do not occur. Because of the great power of its holiness, it does not appear to be holy at all.

THE RUNG OF PRIDE AND HUMILITY

NO DIFFERENT FROM THE REST

Do not tell yourself in your heart of hearts that you are greater than your neighbor, because you serve God so very fervently. You are no different from the rest of the creatures who were created for the service of God. And how could you be more admirable than the worm? For it serves its Maker with all its power and strength.

DO NOT WEIGH

When you talk to people, do not weigh whether or not their thoughts are clinging steadfastly to God. A soul that weighs suffers harm.

ON THE SHORES OF JORDAN

"These are the words which Moses spoke unto all Israel beyond the Jordan, in the wilderness."
Many a man who thinks he harbors God knows nothing of him. And God is close to many a man who thinks he is yearning for God from afar. Now you ought always to feel that you are standing on the shores of Jordan and have not yet entered the land. And even though you have fulfilled many commandments, you ought to realize that you have done nothing.

In the psalms we read: "Mine eyes are ever toward the Lord; for He will bring forth my feet out of the net."

As the bird-catcher who baits a net, and a bird comes and pecks at it and tangles his foot in the cord, so does the Evil Inclination confront men with all the good they have done, their learning, charities, and all manner of devout actions, in order to snare them in the net of pride. But, if the Inclination succeeds, man can free himself no more than the captive bird. Nothing then can save him except the help of God.

HE WHO IS FULL OF HIMSELF

There is no room for God in him who is full of himself.

THE TWO EXTREMES

There are two extremes among men. One sort of man is wholly evil. He knows his Lord, yet deliberately defies him. The other thinks he is wholly righteous, and people take him at his own value. But though he studies and prays incessantly and mortifies his flesh, he toils in vain, for he has no true faith. And this is the difference between them: he who is all evil can be cured of his infirmity when he wakens to the Turning, and turns to

God with a whole heart and begs him to point the way to the light. But that other, who has not the possibility of recognizing the greatness of his Creator and the true nature of service because, in his own eyes, he is righteous—how can he turn?

THE BEES

They say that the proud are reborn as bees. For in his heart the proud man says: "I am a writer, I am a singer, I am a great one at studying." And since what is said of such men is true—that they will not turn to God, not even on the threshold of hell—they are reborn after they die. They are born again as bees that hum and buzz: "I am, I am, I am."

GRAVER THAN ALL SIN

Pride is graver than all sin. For the words which God said of himself hold for sinners: ". . . who dwelleth with them in the midst of their uncleannesses." But our sages tell us that, concerning the proud man, God says: "I and he cannot dwell together in this world."

THE PEG AND THE CROWN

A leader of Israel must not think that the Lord of the world chose him because he is a great man. If the king chose to hang his crown on a wooden peg in the wall, would the peg boast that its beauty drew the gaze of the king to it?

THE FULL STATURE

We say in our prayers: "Every stature shall bow before Thee." Only when man reaches the highest rung, when he reaches his full stature, only then does he become truly humble in his own eyes, and knows what it is: "to bow before Thee."

THE REPROVER AND THE REPROVED

The strength of him who accepts reproof is greater than his who reproves. For if a man humbles himself to accept reproof and to recognize its truth, then God's words apply to him: "I dwell in the high and holy place, with him also that is of a contrite and humble spirit."

THERE AND THERE, TOO

We read in the psalm: "If I ascend up into heaven, Thou art there; if I make my bed in the netherworld, behold, here Thou art." When I consider myself great and think I can touch the sky, I discover that God is the faraway There, and the higher I reach, the farther away he is. But if I make my bed in the depths, if I bow my soul down to the netherworld, there, too, he is with me.

Question: All the commandments are written in the Torah. But humility, which is worth all the other virtues put together, is not stated in the Torah as a commandment. All we read about humility is the words in praise of Moses, saying that he was more humble than all the other people. What is the significance of this silence concerning humility?

Answer: If anyone were humble in order to keep a commandment, he would never attain to true humility. To think humility a commandment is the prompting of Satan. He blows up a man's heart, telling him he is learned and righteous and devout, a master of all good works, and worthy to think himself better than the general run of people, but that thinking so would be proud and impious since the commandment is that he must be humble and put himself on a par with others. And a man who interprets humility as a commandment and keeps it as such only feeds his pride the more in doing so.

FOR LIGHT

It is written: "Pure olive oil beaten for the light." We shall be beaten and bruised, but in order to glow—not to grovel!

105

Everyone must have two pockets, so that he can reach into the one or the other, according to his needs. In his right pocket are to be the words: "For my sake was the world created," and in his left: "I am dust and ashes."

THE MEEKNESS OF MOSES

It is written that Moses was meek above all men. How are we to interpret this? He with whom God spoke face to face and whose work was so mighty—how could he think himself less than all others? The reason is this: during those forty days which Moses spent on the heights, his body had become pure and luminous like that of the attendant angels. After that time, he said to himself: "Of what importance is it, if I, whose body has been purified, give service to God? But one of Israel, who is still clad in his dull and turbid flesh and yet serves God—how much greater he is than I!"

THE RUNG OF REDEMPTION

THE TEARS OF ESAU

In the Midrash it is written: "Messiah, son of David, will not come until the tears of Esau have ceased to flow." The children of Israel, who are God's children, pray for mercy day and night; and shall they weep in vain so long as the children of Esau shed tears? But "the tears of Esau"—that does not mean the tears which the peoples of the earth weep and you do not weep; they are the tears that all human beings weep when they ask something for themselves, and pray for it. And truly: Messiah, son of David, will not come until such tears have ceased to flow, until you weep because the Divine Presence is exiled, and because you yearn for its return.

DELAY

Everyone of Israel should know and consider the fact that he, in the particular way he is made, is unique in the world, and that no one like him has ever been. For if someone like him had already been, there would be no reason for him to be in this world. Actually, everyone is something new in this world, and here he must perfect his particular being, for because it is still imperfect the coming of the Messiah is delayed!

In every generation there are great zaddikim who shirk the work of salvation by devoting themselves to the Torah. As they fulfill the commandments, each of them ponders on the holy place his soul came from, and is intent on having his soul go home to that place after its earthly journey is accomplished, to rejoice in the light of heavenly wisdom. That is why the things of this earth are as nothing to such a man. And though he is saddened by the misery among men and the bitter exile of Israel, these are not enough to move his heart to dare in prayer what must be dared. All his great longing is directed solely to his own homecoming, as it is written: "One generation passeth away, and another generation cometh; and the earth abideth forever. The sun also ariseth and the sun goeth down, and hasteth to his place where he ariseth." Suns rise and go down, and let the misery on earth endure.

FOR THE SAKE OF REDEMPTION

It is written: "And now, lest he put forth his hand, and take also of the tree of life, and eat, and live forever." When the two human beings had committed their first sin, God, in the fulness of his mercy, permitted them to live in the world of death, so that they might find perfect redemption. That is why he decided to prevent them from eating of the tree of life, for then their spirit would never have fought free of matter and prepared for redemption. So he drove them out of the Garden of Eden.

BANISHMENT AND SALVATION

Question: God said to Moses: "Now shalt thou see what I will do to Pharaoh; for by a strong hand shall he let them go, and by a strong hand shall he drive them out of his land." Need the slave who is freed from heavy servitude be driven into freedom? Will he not hasten from it as the bird from the snare?

Answer: When Israel is banished, it is always because it has placed a ban on itself, and only when Israel dissolves this self-imposed ban does it attain salvation. When Israel overcomes the power of evil within itself, the demonic power of evil is broken, and instantly the rulers of earth also lose their power to subjugate Israel. Because Israel in Egypt was not willing to return from spiritual exile, Moses said to the Lord: ". . . neither hast Thou delivered Thy people at all." This means: "It is not you who can deliver them." But God replies: "Now shalt thou see . . ." And he, who is more powerful than all the powers, keeps the covenant. He casts his great light on the demonic power of Egypt and dazzles it. But the holy sparks which were locked in it awake; each finds its kin. The sparks behold the primal light and flame toward it, until the demonic power cannot endure them any longer and is forced to drive them out. And the moment this happens on high, it also happens below, in Israel and in Pharaoh. That is the significance of the plagues.

BASENESS

Question: It is written: "The children of Israel lifted up their eyes and, behold, Egypt was marching after them; and they were sore afraid; and the children of Israel cried out unto the Lord." Why were they so afraid, since they knew that God himself was helping them?

Answer: When they were in Egypt, when they were in baseness up to their ears, they did not see it. But now they lifted up their eyes and saw baseness coming after them. They had thought that, since God had led them out of Egypt, all that was over and done with. Now suddenly they realized that baseness was still with them—and they cried out to God. "And Moses said unto the people: 'Fear ye not, stand still, and see the salvation of the Lord which He will work for you today; for whereas ye have seen Egypt today, ye shall see them again no more for ever. The Lord will fight for you . . .'" Now that you yourselves see that you are base, the Lord will help you out of your

baseness. ". . . And ye shall hold your peace."
Hold your peace, for help has already been
granted you.

OF JOSEPH'S BROTHERS

A man cannot find redemption until he sees the
flaws in his soul, and tries to efface them. Nor can
a people be redeemed until it sees the flaws in its
soul and tries to efface them. But whether it be a
man or a people, whoever shuts out the realization
of his flaws is shutting out redemption. We can
be redeemed only to the extent to which we see
ourselves.

When Jacob's sons said to Joseph: "We are up-
right men," he answered them: "That is it that I
spoke unto you, saying, 'Ye are spies.'" But after
that, when they confessed the truth in their hearts
and with their lips, and said to one another: "We
are verily guilty concerning our brother," the first
sparks of their redemption were kindled, Joseph
was overwhelmed with compassion; he "turned
himself about from them, and wept."

THE FALSE MESSIAHS

Once there was an emperor whose only son fell
ill. One physician advised them to spread an acrid
salve on a piece of linen and wrap it around the
bare body of the patient. Another contradicted
him, saying that the boy was too weak to bear the

great pain the salve would cause. A third prescribed a sleeping potion, but the fourth feared it might prove injurious to the patient's heart. Then the fifth suggested that they give the prince a spoonful whenever he woke and was in pain. And so it was done.

When God saw that the soul of Israel had sickened, he wrapped it in the acrid linen of the Exile, and, that the soul might bear the pain, he swathed it in numbing sleep. But lest the sleep destroy the soul, he wakes it from time to time with hope in a false Messiah, and then lulls it to rest again until the night will be past and the true Messiah will appear. And for the same reason, even the eyes of sages are sometimes blinded.

ON THE DAY OF DESTRUCTION

Question: Why should the Messiah be born on the anniversary of the destruction of the Temple—as the tradition has it?

Answer: The kernel which is sown in the earth must disintegrate so that the ear of grain may sprout from its pieces. Strength cannot be resurrected until it has dwelt in deep secrecy. Putting off a shape, putting on a shape—these are done in the instant of pure nothingness. In the husk of forgetting grows the power of memory. That is the power of redemption. On the day of destruction, power lies at the bottom of the deep and grows. That is why, on the anniversary of the destruction of the Temple, we sit on the ground. That is why on that day we visit graves. That is why on that day the Messiah is to be born.

LABOR PAINS

If a pregnant woman goes into labor in the eighth month, when her time is not yet come, doctors try to stop her labor. But not so in the ninth month. If the woman goes into labor then, doctors try to increase it, so that she may soon give birth. That is why, formerly, when people called to heaven, begging God to free the earth of some misery, their prayer was granted, for the time was not yet come. But now that redemption is near, no prayer which ascends in behalf of the sorrowful world is of avail, but sorrow is heaped upon sorrow, so that the birth may soon be accomplished.

THE THREE PILLARS

Three pillars support the world: teaching, service, and good deeds, and, as the world approaches its end, the first two will shrink, and only good deeds will grow. And then what is written will become truth: "Zion shall be redeemed with justice."

In the last three hours of the world before Redemption, it will be as difficult to cling to Jewishness as to climb a smooth wall of ice. That is why in the prayer we find the words: "Help us during the three hours." Those are the last hours.

THE KINGDOM OF GOD

Those who do not walk in loneliness will be bewildered when the Messiah comes and they are called. But we will be as one who has been asleep and whose spirit is quiet and calm.

IN FREE SPACE

In free space there is neither right nor left. In the same way, there is reward and punishment only in this, and not in the Messianic world.

THE END OF PRAYERS

At the close of the Seventy-second Psalm are the words: "And let the whole earth be filled with His glory. Amen, and Amen. The prayers of David, the son of Jesse are ended." All prayers and hymns are a plea for His glory to be revealed throughout the world. But if once the whole earth is indeed filled with it, there will be no further need to pray.

NOTES AND INDEX

NOTES

Page 13 *Our God* . . . : Introductory phrase in many prayers.

13 *God of Abraham* . . . . : Introductory phrase in the Prayer of Benedictions.

14 *And Israel saw:* Exod. 14:31.

15 *Put off thy shoes:* Exod. 3:5.

15 *I shall hide, hide:* cf. Deut. 31:18.

15 *I saw all Israel:* I Kings 22:17.

16 *Thou art My son:* Ps. 2:7.

17 *Where is the place:* From the sanctification (*Kedushah*) during the Sabbath Service.

17 *Where shall I find you:* Quoted in a hymn by Judah ha-Levi.

17 *The whole earth:* Isa. 6:3.

17 *Speak thou with us:* Exod. 20:16.

17 *Fear not:* Exod. 20:17.

18 *Then Jacob was greatly afraid:* Gen. 32:8.

18 *In the day:* Gen. 5:1.

18 *I stood between:* Deut. 5:5.

19 *I am my beloved's:* Cant. 7:11.

19 *When any man:* Lev. 1:2.

19 *How long:* Ps. 13:3.

20 *I am JHWH:* Exod. 20:2.

21 *Oh that thou wert:* Cant. 8:1.

22 *Thou shalt make thee:* Exod. 34:17.

22 *Know what is above you:* Sayings of the Fathers, II.1.

22 *And upon the likeness:* Ezek. 1:26.

22 *To whom then will ye liken Me:* Isa. 40:25.

Page 23 *Noah walked:* Gen. 6:9.

23 *And the earth:* Isa. 66:1.

THE RUNG OF PRAYER

Page 29 *Lord . . . of the world:* Introductory phrase in many benedictions.

29 *But they that wait:* Isa. 40:31.

30 *For singing to our God:* Ps. 147:1.

30 *An altar of earth:* Exod. 20:24-25.

31 *Ye shall serve:* Exod. 23:25.

31 *"Section of Praise" (Perek Shirah):* a compilation of scriptural verses in praise of God, which all living things recite, each chanting its own special verse.

32 *He is thy psalm:* cf. Deut. 10:21.

THE RUNG OF HEAVEN AND EARTH

Page 37 *The heavens:* Ps. 115:16.

37 *Man, his origin:* Prayer recited during the Days of Awe.

39 *The tree of life:* Gen. 2:9.

40 *And he stood:* cf. Gen. 18-8.

41 *And to walk hidden:* cf. Mic. 6:8.

42 *Who healeth:* Ps. 147:3.

42 *The sacrifices:* Ps. 51:19.

43 *The Divine Presence:* Babylonian Talmud, Shabbat 30b.

44 *Rejoice the soul:* Ps. 86:4.

THE RUNG OF SERVICE

Page 49 *And there was evening:* Gen. 1:5.

50 *Rashi:* Rabbi Solomon ben Isaac of Troyes, died 1105, the classical commentator upon the Bible and the Babylonian Talmud.

Page 50 *I appeared unto Abraham:* Exod. 6:3.

50 *Simeon ben Yohai:* great talmudic master of the second century.

51 *Open to me:* Ps. 118:19.

51 *Thou hast begun:* Deut. 3:24.

51 *As a beginning:* cf. Gen. 1:1.

52 *Cast me not off:* Ps. 71:9.

52 *They are new:* Lam. 3:23.

52 *We will do:* cf. Exod. 24:7.

53 *And Abel:* Gen. 4:4.

53 *Midrash:* exposition, homiletic exegesis of Scripture. *Midrashim* are collections of such exegeses.

53 *I shall not die:* Ps. 118:17.

56 *Hillel:* one of the early talmudic masters (1st cent., B.C.E.).

56 *If I am not for myself:* Sayings of the Fathers, I. 14.

THE RUNG OF THE TEACHINGS

Page 59 *And the mountain:* Deut. 4:11.

59 *And this shall be:* Exod. 3:12.

60 *It went on no more:* Deut. 5:19.

60 *Now, therefore:* cf. Exod. 19:5.

60 *Feast of Revelation:* = Feast of Weeks; see p. 59.

61 *When the Lord:* cf. Ps. 126:1.

61 *Abbayyi and Raba:* leading talmudic teachers in Babylonia during the fourth century.

62 *When a word is spoken:* Babylonian Talmud, Yebamot 97a.

62 *And ye shall be:* Exod. 19:6.

62 *Rashi: see* note to p. 50.

62 *Those who are perfect:* Babylonian Talmud, Berakhot 34b.

63 *Take heed:* Deut. 4:23.

THE RUNG OF THE WAY

THE RUNG OF LOVE

THE RUNG OF GOOD AND EVIL

THE RUNG OF PRIDE AND HUMILITY

THE RUNG OF REDEMPTION

INDEX TO THE SAYINGS

126